Introduction

The stories at Stage 6 continue the adventures of Biff, Chip, Kipper and friends. The magic key device enables the stories to incorporate adventure and fantasy within a safe setting. The introduction of new vocabulary and the sentence structures continue to be controlled, and key words from previous stages are frequently used in the stories.

Stage 6 continues the ongoing adventures of the children and the magic key that began at Stage 4. It is recommended that children begin with the first four stories at Stage 6. The other two stories can be read in any order. The Stage 7 stories can also be read in any order although *The Lost Key* contains pictorial references to the other three stories in Stage 7.

At this level, it is still important to introduce the story through discussion, to enable children to read the texts with increasing confidence and independence. The sight vocabulary the children have gained in the earlier stages provides a platform for children to combine their knowledge of letter sounds and word meanings to interpret new words as they meet them in these stories. Words from the NLS high frequency word list are also used, so children can learn these words as sight vocabulary.

How to introduce the books

At Stages 6 and 7 it is still important to introduce the stories before independent reading. This will give the children sufficient information about the context and setting to enable them to read with confidence and independence.

Before reading the story, talk about the cover and the title. Read the back cover blurb and ask them to predict what the story is about. Go through the book together, looking at the pictures and talking about them. Point out and read any new context words that might prove difficult.

This booklet provides suggestions for using the books in group and independent reading activities. Prompts and ideas are provided for introducing and reading each book with a child or group of children. Suggestions are also provided for writing, speaking and listening and cross-curricular links. You can use these suggestions to follow on from your reading, or use at another time.

Take-Home Cards are also available for each book. These provide friendly prompts and suggestions for parents reading with their children. You can store the relevant card with each book in your 'Take-Home' selection of titles.

Reading skills

Stages 6 and 7 develop:
- strategies for independent reading, including consolidation of irregular phonological and spelling patterns
- insights into feelings and motivation of characters
- a wider sight vocabulary
- awareness of other viewpoints
- confidence through familiarity with the characters and the format
- sustained independent writing.

Teaching Notes

Contents

In the Garden

Kipper and the Giant

The Outing

Land of the Dinosaurs

Robin Hood

The Treasure Chest

Vocabulary chart

In the Garden	Year 2 High frequency words	be called came can't do don't down good got had help here his house love must now off out over pull(ed) push(ed) ran so that them there too took very want were what with
	Context words	bottle bumble-bee climb desert drops flowerpot giant grass inside jungle mountain outside paw rain sandpit slugs strawberries
Kipper and the Giant	Year 2 High frequency words	again an another back be boy but called came don't good got have help here house little lived not now old one out over people put ran saw so than their time took us very want what when with
	Context words	adventure angry bigger castle giant mend nobody outside pointed programme roofs signpost stamped stone threw tiny towards village
The Outing	Year 2 High frequency words	about an back called came don't good got had help here his home house make off one our out push ran school so some that them time too took were what when with
	Context words	apatosaurus camera couldn't crocodiles didn't dinosaurs elephants hope lady lions model museum near photograph pictures rain room shoe showed silly tickets toilet told water zoo
Land of the Dinosaurs	Year 2 High frequency words	an another be by called came could did don't down good got had have help here house just little must not off one out put ran school some take that time took us very want water went were what
	Context words	apatosaurus camera climbed crack dinosaurs didn't dragon-fly eat enormous fierce film flew footprint found hatch hide hill hurt land long meet museum photograph picked silly won't
Robin Hood	Year 2 High frequency words	about again an back black by called came can't could do don't down good got had help her here him his how just lived made must new next not one out over people put ran saw seen so some take that them there three time too took us want(ed) went what where who will with
	Context words	Anneena catch cheer free grabbed guitar lock nobody pantomime part recorder sang Sheriff song suddenly village wood

Vocabulary chart

The Treasure Chest	Year 2 High frequency words	about after an been but called came did do don't down good had how little many more new next now off old our out over pull(ed) push(ed) put ran saw seen some ten than that them then there time too took very want water were what who with
	Context words	air blew bubbles close colours couldn't dangerous didn't different flippers jellyfish lengths lovely masks necklace octopus passed shark surprise swam swimming tanks test thought treasure underwater
Red Planet	Year 2 High frequency words	about again an as back be but called came do don't down five four from good had here his home how just little made may must not off one over out people pull(ed) put ran red saw so some take that them then there these three time too took trees two us want(ed) way were what where will with
	Context words	boots broken buggy button computer crash dust float floor mountains paw pieces planet pretended rocket safe space spaceman spacesuit
Lost in the Jungle	Year 2 High frequency words	as be been but called came could did don't down good got had have help her here home house how if jump(ed) just last little love made may not one out over pull(ed) put ran saw so some ten that their them there time too took tree us way water were what where with
	Context words	air alligators angry animals asleep behind bigger birthday broken building catch chocolates city explorers fell found full gold greenhouse hanging jungle know lady lost might mind monkey place plants presents river safe shook snake stay steps through throw trap wake waterfall wonderful years
The Broken Roof	Year 2 High frequencywords	about after again as back been but called can't could did do don't down first from got had have her home house how if just little made may name new not now old one our out over push(ed) put ran saw school so some take that their them then there these time three took two very want water were what when who will your
	Context words	asked books broken bucket climbed clothes cook display dumped fell fence field find funny handle hole junk kitchen know long mangle mend mother picture rocking roof secret sheet silly sorry swap tea table through upset washing worked workmen

Vocabulary chart

The Lost Key	Year 2 High frequency words	about again as back bed been boy(s) but by called came can't could do don't down from good had has have help her here him his home house how if just last little make man may must new next not now off old one our out over pull(ed) put ran saw seen so some take that their them then there time took two very want way were what where who will with would
	Context words	air asked broken buy clang crash didn't fast fault fell flew found glass grass greenhouse junk lady lost mend mower painted pictures pocket rain remind rocket round rubbed sold sorry spun started string swings threw through tied told trainers wouldn't

Curriculum coverage chart

	Speaking and listening	Reading	Writing
In the Garden			
NLS Y2 T1/NC	3a, 3e	W2, W5, W6, S3, T2, T4	T11
Scotland	Level A	Level A	Level A
N. Ireland	Activities: a, e, f, g Outcomes: a, b, c, d	Activities: a, b, c, e Outcomes: b, c, d	Outcomes: a, b, c, e
Wales	Range: 1, 2, 3 Skills: 1, 2, 3, 4, 5, 6	Range: 1, 2, 4, 5, 6 Skills: 1, 2	Range: 1, 2, 3, 4, 5 Skills: 1, 4, 5, 8
Kipper and the Giant			
NLS Y2 T1/NC	1c, 1e, 4b	W2, W5, W6, S2, S3, T5	T11
Scotland	Level A	Level A	Level A
N. Ireland	Activities: a, b, c, e, f Outcomes: a, b, c, e	Activities: a, b, c Outcomes: a, b, c, d, f	Outcomes: a, b, c, e
Wales	Range: 1, 2, 3, 5 Skills: 1, 2, 3	Range: 1, 2, 4, 5, 6 Skills: 1, 2	Range: 1, 2, 3, 4, 7 Skills: 1, 2, 4, 7, 8
The Outing			
NLS Y2 T1/NC	3a, 3d	W4, S3, T2, T3, T5	T10
Scotland	Level A	Level A	Level A
N. Ireland	Activities: a, b, f, h Outcomes: a, b, c, d, e	Activities: a, b, c, e Outcomes: b, c, d, e, f	Outcomes: a, b, c, h, i
Wales	Range: 1, 2, 3 Skills: 1, 2, 3, 4, 5	Range: 1, 2, 4, 5, 6 Skills: 1, 2	Range: 1, 2, 3, 4, 5 Skills: 1, 3, 4, 7, 8
Land of the Dinosaurs			
NLS Y2 T1/NC	1e, 4b	W5, W6, W8, S3, S4, T11	T11
Scotland	Level A	Level A	Level A
N. Ireland	Activities: a, b, c, e, g Outcomes: a, b, c, d, e	Activities: a, b, c, e Outcomes: b, c, d, e, f	Outcomes: a, b, c, e
Wales	Range: 1, 2, 3, 5 Skills: 1, 2, 3, 4, 5	Range: 1, 2, 4, 5, 6 Skills: 1, 2	Range: 1, 2, 3 Skills: 1, 2, 3, 6, 7, 8
Robin Hood			
NLS Y2 T1/NC	1e, 4b	W3, W5, W6, S5, T2, T4	T11
Scotland	Level A	Level A	Level A
N. Ireland	Activities: a, b, c, e Outcomes: a, b, c, d, e	Activities: a, b, c, e Outcomes: b, c, d, e, f	Outcomes: b, c, e
Wales	Range: 1, 2, 3, 5 Skills: 1, 2, 3, 4	Range: 1, 2, 4, 5, 6 Skills: 1, 2	Range: 1, 2, 3, 4, 5 Skills: 1, 2, 3, 7, 8
The Treasure Chest			
NLS Y2 T1/NC	1d, 1e	W5, W6, W9, S3, S6, T2, T5	T15
Scotland	Level A	Level A	Level A
N. Ireland	Activities: a, e, f Outcomes: a, b, c, d, e	Activities: a, b, e, f Outcomes: b, c, d, f	Outcomes: b, c, d
Wales	Range: 1, 2, 3, 5 Skills: 1, 2, 3, 4, 5, 6	Range: 1, 2, 4, 5, 6 Skills: 1, 2, 3	Range: 1, 2, 3, 5, 7 Skills: 1, 2, 7, 8

Curriculum coverage chart

Red Planet			
NLS Y2 T2/NC	4a, 4b	W4, W5, S6, S7, T5	T14
Scotland	Level A	Level A	Level A
N. Ireland	Activities: a, b, c, e, f Outcomes: a, b, c, d, e	Activities: a, b, c, e, f Outcomes: b, c, d, e, f, g	Outcomes: a, b, h, i
Wales	Range: 1, 2, 3, 5 Skills: 1, 2, 3	Range: 1, 2, 4, 5, 6 Skills: 1, 2	Range: 1, 2, 4, 7 Skills: 1, 2, 3, 4, 5, 6
Lost in the Jungle			
NLS Y2 T2/NC	1d, 2d	W4, W6, W7, S2, S5, T5	T13
Scotland	Level A	Level A	Level A
N. Ireland	Activities: a, b, f, g Outcomes: a, b, c, d, e	Activities: a, b, c, e, f Outcomes: b, c, d, e, f, h	Outcomes: a, b, c
Wales	Range: 1, 3 Skills: 1, 2, 3	Range: 1, 2, 3, 4, 5 Skills: 1, 2, 3	Range: 1, 2, 5, 6 Skills: 1, 2, 3, 4, 7, 8
The Broken Roof			
NLS Y2 T2/NC	1d, 1e	W5, S2, T2, T5, T6	T13
Scotland	Level A	Level A	Level A
N. Ireland	Activities: a, b, e, f, g Outcomes: a, b, c, d, e	Activities: a, b, c, e, f Outcomes: b, c, d, e, f	Outcomes: a, b, c
Wales	Range: 1, 2, 3 Skills: 1, 2, 3, 4, 5, 6	Range: 1, 2, 3, 4, 5 Skills: 1, 2	Range: 1, 2, 3, 5, 7 Skills: 1, 2, 3, 7, 8
The Lost Key			
NLS Y2 T2/NC	1d, 4b	W6, W7, W8, S2, S7, T2, T4	T13
Scotland	Level A	Level A	Level A
N. Ireland	Activities: a, b, c, f, g Outcomes: a, b, c, e	Activities: a, b, c, e, f Outcomes: b, c, d, e, f	Outcomes: a, b, c, e
Wales	Range: 1, 2, 3, 4, 5 Skills: 1, 2, 3	Range: 1, 2, 4, 5, 6 Skills: 1, 2	Range: 1, 2, 3, 4, 5, 7 Skills: 1, 4, 7, 8

In the Garden

Before reading

- Look at the front cover. Ask the children: *Do you think the grass and flowers are big, or are the children small?*
- Read the title together.
- Look at the illustrations through the story and talk about what is happening.

During reading

- Ask the children to read the story. Praise and encourage them while they read, and prompt as necessary.
- As you listen to individual children, ask questions about the story to ensure they understand what is happening, e.g. on page 11 ask, *Why did Kipper say "Oh no!" when Biff suggested they go down to the "desert"?*
- If children have difficulty reading compound words, e.g. "sandpit", "flowerpot", encourage them to find smaller words within them.

Observing Check that the children:

- ■ read high frequency words with confidence (W5/6)
- ■ use a range of strategies to work out new words (T2).

Group and independent reading activities

Text level work

Objective To understand time and sequential relationships in stories (T4).

You will need to write these three sentences on the board:

They came to a mountain.
Floppy chased the cat away.
The children were in the grass.

- Ask the children to say the order in which the above events happened in the story, using "First", "Next", "Last".
- Ask the children to choose three other sentences from the story to say what happened and write them using "First", "Next", "Last".

Observing Do the children choose sentences that show a sequence of events?
Do the children remember to use capital letters and full stops?

Sentence level work

Objective   To recognise and take account of commas and exclamation marks in reading aloud with appropriate expression (S3).

● Look at page 8 with the children. Ask them to point to the exclamation mark in the text and to suggest how that sentence should be read.

● Ask the children to read pages 8 to 17, with a partner, each child reading alternate pages. Tell them to read the words in the way they think the characters would say them, taking into account any commas or exclamation marks they see.

Observing   Do the children use an expressive voice when sentences end with exclamation marks?
Do they understand that the text within the speech marks should be read more expressively than other sections of the text?

Word level work

Objective   To revise and extend the reading and spelling of words containing spellings of long vowel phonemes (W2).

● Write these words on the board and discuss their sounds and spelling patterns: name, play, train ("ai"); bee, seat, feet ("ee").

● Ask the children to look through the story and find six other words that have the same vowel sounds and spelling patterns. (Choose from the following: "ai": playing, came, away, chased, ate, rain; "ee": key, strawberries, eat, feel, see.)

Observing   Do the children recognise words with the same sound but different spelling?

Speaking and listening activities

Objective   Take turns in speaking (3a), give reasons for opinions and actions (3e).

- Ask the children to imagine they are as tiny as the characters in the story.
- Talk about how the characters felt when they saw the insects, climbed the sandpit and tried to find their way through the grass. What word did the characters use for the grass?
- One at a time, ask the children to describe to the group what it would be like to be tiny in their own garden or the park. Ask each child to say something that would be fun, and something that would be scary or dangerous.

Writing

Objective   To use language of time to structure a sequence of events (T11).

- Ask the children to retell the story, thinking about how they say what happened and when.
- Write some time language on the board, e.g. "First...", "Meanwhile...", "After...", "Suddenly...", "At last...".
- Ask the children to write what it would be like to be tiny in their own garden, or in a park, using the language of time to show the sequence of events.

Cross-curricular link
◄► Maths: Measures, shape and space

Kipper and the Giant

Before reading

- Look at the front cover together. Ask the children to read the title and the blurb on the back cover. Ask the children: *Who do you think will be the giant in the story?*
- Look briefly through the story up to page 9 to confirm the children's ideas.

During reading

- Ask the children to read the story. Praise and encourage them while they read, and prompt as necessary.
- As you listen to individual children, ask them questions about the story, for example ask: *Why do you think Kipper is frightened?* (page 6); *Why don't the people like Kipper? Did he do anything wrong?* (pages 10 and 11).

Observing Check that the children:

- read high frequency words on sight (W5/6)
- read with expression appropriate to the grammar and punctuation (S3)
- understand the reasons why Kipper wasn't liked by the villagers, at first (T5).

Group and independent reading activities

Text level work

Objective To identify and discuss reasons for events in stories linked to plot (T5).

You will need to write some questions about the story on the board:

Why did Kipper run to get Biff?
Why did Kipper go to the village?
Why did Kipper begin to cry?
Why did the villagers say "Good Old Kipper"?
Why was the giant very angry?

- Ask the children, in pairs, to look through the book to find the answers to the questions and discuss them together.
- Ask each child to write a new question, swap it with his/her partner's question, and then write the answer to the partner's question, referring to the book if necessary.

Are the children able to identify the reasons for the things Kipper does in the story?

Sentence level work

Objective To find examples of words and phrases that link sentences (S2).

- Discuss with the children the sorts of words that can be used to join sentences and show a sequence of events, e.g. "next", "then", "before", "after". Together, draw up a list of words the children can use in their own writing.
- Write on the board "Kipper went to the village."
- Ask the children to write what happens next in the story, using words from the list to link their sentences.

Observing Do the children remember to begin each sentence with a capital letter?

Word level work

Objective To revise and extend the reading and spelling of words containing different spellings of long vowel phonemes (W2).

You will need poster paper.

- Write the word "Giant" on the board. Discuss the "ie" sound. Ask the children to collect words from the story with the same long vowel sound, and group them according to spelling pattern, e.g. "i-e": like, time, inside, outside; "igh": frightened; "y": cry, try; "i": find, tiny.
- Transfer these words under their headings onto the poster paper.
- Ask the children to think of other words with the same spelling patterns from their own experience and list these on the poster.
- Display the poster in the classroom and ask the children to add new words to it when they find them.

Observing Can the children differentiate between long and short vowel sounds and spellings?

Speaking and listening activities

Objectives Organise what they say (1c); include relevant detail (1e); create and sustain roles individually and when working with others (4b).

- Choose some children to take turns to be Kipper and sit in the "hot seat".
- Encourage the other children to ask "Kipper" questions to describe what it is like to be a giant and why he does the things he does in the story.

Writing

Objective To use language of time to structure a sequence of events (T11).

- Ask the children to imagine they are giants and they have come to visit the school.
- Ask them to describe what they see, how it is different from normal and what difficulties they encounter, e.g. low doorways, tiny chairs. Allow the children to role play being a giant if it helps them to describe the actions.
- Ask the children to write a description of their visit to the school as a giant.

Cross-curricular link
◀▶ RE: Revision of beliefs and practice: the story of David and Goliath

The Outing

Before reading

- Look at the front cover together and discuss what is happening. Ask the children to read the back cover blurb and say what they think will happen in the story.
- Ask the children to briefly look through the book to see where the characters go.

During reading

- Ask the children to read the story. Praise and encourage them while they read, and prompt as necessary.
- Encourage the children to use the picture clues to work out new words.
- If children struggle with the word "apatosaurus" on page 15, ask them to break it down into syllables.

Observing Check that the children:

- read with expression appropriate to the grammar and punctuation (S3)
- use a range of strategies to work out new words (T2)
- understand why the characters went to the museum (T5).

Group and independent reading activities

Text level work

Objective To be aware of the difference between spoken and written language through comparing oral recounts with text (T3).

- Ask the children to work with a partner and to take turns to re-tell the story to each other. The children then look through the text and compare their versions.
- Ask some children to say their versions of the story to the group and discuss the differences between the re-tellings. The other children could point out the parts of the re-tellings that used the same or almost the same wording as the book version.

Observing Are the children able to re-tell the story without using sentences from the book?

Do the children recognise that their re-tellings do not use formal story language?

Sentence level work

Objective To recognise and take account of commas and exclamation marks in reading aloud with appropriate expression (S3).

- Ask the children to work with a partner and to take turns to read only the spoken words. Encourage them to use expression appropriate to the punctuation used in the text.
- As a group discuss what helps the children to read with expression, e.g. exclamation marks.

Observing Do the children pause at commas and change their tone when speech ends with an exclamation mark?

Word level work

Objective To investigate and classify words with the same sounds but different spellings (W4).

You will need to write these sentences with missing words on the board:

"We're going...the zoo."
"Don't go...near the water."
We all wear...shoes.

- Discuss the three ways to spell "to", "too", "two" with the children.
- Ask the children to read the sentences on the board, then write them, filling in each gap with the correct word.
- Ask them to read through the book and find two ways the word is spelt in the story.
- Can the children write three new sentences using the different spellings?

Observing Do the children understand the different uses of these words that sound alike but are spelt differently?

Speaking and listening activities

Objectives Take turns in speaking (3a); extend their ideas in the light of discussion (3d).

- Sit with the children in a circle and discuss what Wilf did near the water on page 6 of the story.
- Ask the children to think about the dangers of water and, in turn, contribute one idea about playing near water.

Cross-curricular link
◀▶ PSHE: Developing a healthy safer lifestyle

Writing

Objective To use story structure to write about own experience in same/similar form (T10).

- Ask the children to tell you what happened in the story, and scribe a simplified version on the board.
- Discuss which parts of the simplified story would stay the same if it were being written about different children and using a different outing.
- Using the parts identified by the children, write them as a framework to help the children structure their own writing.
- Ask the children to use the framework to write about an outing on which they have been.

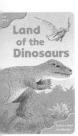

Land of the Dinosaurs

Before reading

- Look at the cover together. Read the title and ask the children to read the blurb on the back cover.
- Ask them to say what they think will happen in the story.

During reading

- Ask the children to read the story. Praise and encourage them while they read, and prompt as necessary. Encourage the children to read with expression.
- As you listen to individual children, ask them questions to help their understanding of this story and its link with the previous story, e.g. *Why is Wilf wearing a plastic bag on one foot?* (page 14); *Why do you think the dinosaur looks startled on page 16? Why won't Biff have any photographs of the dinosaurs from her camera?* (page 24).

Observing Check that the children:

- read high frequency words with fluency and confidence (W5/6)
- take account of the grammar and punctuation while reading aloud (S3).

Group and independent reading activities

Text level work

Objective To use the language of time to structure a sequence of events (T11).

You will need the following word cards:

Firstly, Immediately, Meanwhile, After that, Suddenly, Next, Then;

and these sentence strips:

A dinosaur flew down.
Nadim found some eggs.
Chip found a footprint.
Wilf ran on and climbed a hill.
Biff took a photograph.
A little dinosaur came out of the egg.
Biff picked up a stick.

- Ask the children to put the sentence strips in the right order, and to start each one with one of the word cards.

- Alternatively, put the words and sentences into word processing software and ask the children to drag and drop the words into the sentences.

Observing Do the children need to refer to the story to sequence the sentences?

Sentence level work

Objective To re-read own writing for sense and punctuation (S4).

- Ask the children to look through the book at the illustrations and choose the one they like best.
- Tell them to write two new sentences for the picture.
- Ask them to read their sentences aloud and to check they make sense.

Observing Do the children begin their sentences with capital letters and end with full stops?

Word level work

Objective To secure understanding and use of the term "vowel" (W8).

- Ask the children to look through the story and find words with one, two, three and four vowels in them.
- Can they find a word with more than four vowels?
- To illustrate the importance of vowels, list one or two words that the children found on the board, rub out the vowels within each word, and ask the children to try to pronounce the words.

Observing Do the children scan the text to select words by length?
Do they realise that vowels are crucial letters of a word?

Speaking and listening activities

Objectives Include relevant detail (1e); create and sustain roles individually (4b).

- Talk about what Biff does when the dinosaur egg hatches.
- Ask the children to take turns to be Biff and sit in the "hot seat".
- Ask the other children to think of a question to ask "Biff" about what she did.

Writing

Objective To use language of time to structure a sequence of events (T11).

You will need word cards of time connectives.

- Ask the children, in pairs, to discuss the story and to pick six key events to write a sentence about. They may need to use the book to help them.
- Tell the children to pick a word card to begin their sentences, so that the sentences show the sequence of the key events.

Robin Hood

Before reading

- Look at the cover with the children. Ask them what they think the story is about.
- Read the title and ask them to read the blurb on the back cover.
- Discuss what the children know about Robin Hood and what they think will happen in the story.

During reading

- Ask the children to read the story. Praise and encourage them while they read, and prompt as necessary.
- Discuss why "is" is written in bold print on page 9 and compare this with the text about Robin Hood on page 2.

Observing Check that the children:

- read high frequency words with fluency and confidence (W5/6)
- use a range of strategies to work out new words (T2).

Group and independent reading activities

Text level work

Objective To understand time and sequential relationships in stories, i.e. what happened when (T4).

- Write "What happened when..." on the board.
- Ask the children: *When is the first time Biff sings a song about Robin Hood? Why do you think she sang it?* If necessary, talk about how the characters had been to see the pantomime about Robin Hood the night before.
  How do we know it is the next day when she sang the song?
  Prompt the children to look at the words "The next day" on page 4.
- Ask the children to work with a partner and to think of questions beginning with the words "What happened when..." to ask their partner. Their partner then finds the answer in the book. Ensure the children alternate between asking and answering questions.

Observing Do the children understand that what the characters do affects the plot?
Do they realise that the timing of an event occurs because of what has happened before?

Cross-curricular link
◀▶ Music: Exploring instruments and symbols

Sentence level work

Objective To revise knowledge about other uses of capitalisation and begin to use in own writing (S5).

- Ask the children to look at page 1 of the book and find the words in the picture that are written in capital letters (THEATRE, TONIGHT, ROBIN HOOD).
- Discuss reasons for writing words in capital letters.
- Ask the children to list all the words written in this way that they see around the school and in the classroom.

Observing Do the children understand that using capital letters makes words stand out?

Word level work

Objective To identify the common spelling patterns for the vowel phoneme "oo" (short as in "good") (W3).

- Discuss the "oo" sound in "Robin Hood" with the children.
- Ask them to find other words in the story with the same spelling, e.g. "good", "wood", "took", "looked", "goodbye"; "Woooooooh", "too".
- Discuss the differences in the "oo" sound between some of the words, e.g. short phoneme "oo" as is "good" and long "oo" as in "too". Write the words that the children found in two lists.
- Ask the children to use word banks or dictionaries to find and group other words with the same spelling but different sounds.

Observing Do the children add the new words that they find to the right list?

Speaking and listening activities

Objectives Include relevant detail (1e); create and sustain roles individually (4b).

- Ask some children, in turn, to take the role of Kipper and sit in the "hot seat".
- Ask "Kipper" to tell the group what happened when he met Robin Hood.

Writing

Objective To use language of time to structure a sequence of events (T11).

You will need to write the following time connectives on the board: firstly, then, after that, suddenly.

- Ask the children to turn to the pages in the story that outline how Kipper rescued everyone in the story.
- Ask the children to use the illustrations on pages 18 to 21 as a stimulus and write how Kipper set everyone free. Remind them to use the time connectives to sequence the events.

The Treasure Chest

Before reading

- Look at the cover with the children. Ask them what they think the story is about.
- Read the title and ask them to read the blurb on the back cover.
- Ask the children: *What do you think will happen in the story? Do you think the children will meet an octopus?*

During reading

- Ask the children to read the story. Praise and encourage them while they read, and prompt as necessary.
- On page 17 ask the children what is happening in the illustration. Ask them to read the word "different" and say how this adventure is different.
- Ask why the text says "thought" instead of "said" on page 19.

Observing Check that the children:

- ■ read high frequency words with fluency (W5/6)
- ■ read with expression appropriate to the grammar and punctuation (S3)
- ■ use a variety of cues to decipher new words (T2).

Group and independent reading activities

Text level work

Objective To identify and discuss reasons for events in stories, linked to plot (T5).

- Ask the children to think about three key things that happen in the story, and list them on the board, e.g. the children pass a swimming test; Biff and Chip go shopping for their fish tank; the children have an underwater adventure.
- Ask each child to choose one event and write the reason the event happened, using the word "because" in his/her sentence.

Observing Do the children understand that using "because" shows cause and effect?

Sentence level work

Objective To use a variety of simple organisational devices, e.g. arrows, to indicate sequences and relationships (S6).

You will need photocopies of these sentences from the story written in random order.

The magic began to work.
They saw an octopus sitting on a chest.
They swam up to the ship.
The children could swim under water.
They saw a ship under the water.
The octopus swam away.
It was full of gold.
The children opened the chest.

● Give out the sheets to the children. Ask them to read the sentences and join the events with arrows to show the sequence in which they occur in the story.
● Can the children write a sentence that follows on from the last sentence in the sequence?

Observing Do the children need to refer to the story to work out the right sequence?
Are they able to think of a further sentence without referring to the text?

Word level work

Objective To spell common irregular words, e.g. colour names (W9).

● Ask the children to look at the illustrations on pages 18 and 19.
● Ask them to name and write down the different colours they see. Some children may need to use a dictionary or word bank.

Observing Are the children familiar with the common colour names?
Do the children attempt to spell the words independently?

Speaking and listening activities

Objectives Focus on the main point (1d); include relevant detail (1e).

- Sit with the children in a circle. Ask the children if they can guess who is missing from this adventure.
- Ask them to take turns to suggest a reason why and how Kipper feels.
- Talk about safety in water.

Cross-curricular link
◀▶ PE: Swimming activities and water safety

Writing

Objective To write simple instructions (T15).

- Discuss the swimming test that the characters took on pages 4–6 of the story.
- Ask the children to write some instructions of what the characters had to do to pass the test.
- Scribe some of their suggestions on the board, using a numbered list, e.g. The Swimming Test
  1. Jump into the pool.
  2. Swim 10 lengths.
- Can the children think of other swimming test instructions to put on the end of the list?

Red Planet

Before reading

- Hide the title and look at the cover together. Ask the children: *What do you think the children are looking at?*
- Read the title together and ask the children to read the back cover blurb.
- Look briefly through the story at the illustrations and talk about what is happening.

During reading

- Ask the children to read the story. Praise and encourage them while they read, and prompt as necessary.
- As you listen to individual children, ask them to show you the spoke words in the story and point out the speech marks.

Observing Check that the children:

- ■ recognise the smaller words in the compound words "spacemen" and "spacesuit" (W4)
- ■ identify where speech marks are used to show dialogue (S6).

Group and independent reading activities

Text level work

Objective To discuss story settings; to compare differences; to locate key word and phrases in the text; to consider how different settings influence events and behaviour (T5).

- Discuss the settings in the beginning, middle and end of the story with the children.
- Write the two settings on the board: "The garden", "The red planet"
- Ask the children to work with a partner, and, under the headings, write down their ideas about how the things the children do and se are the same or different.
- Ask them to share their ideas and give reasons for them.

Observing Do the children locate evidence in the text to support their ideas?

Sentence level work

To investigate and recognise a range of other ways of presenting text, e.g. speech bubbles (S7).

You will need six pieces of paper cut in the shape of speech bubbles for each child.

● Ask the children to focus on the illustrations of Floppy on pages 3, 10, 15, 18, 20 and 28.
● Ask them to read the parts that say what Floppy is thinking and to write what they think he would say in the speech bubbles.

Observing Do the children leave out the speech marks when writing in speech bubbles?

Word level work

Objective To discriminate, orally, syllables in multi-syllabic words using children's names and words from their reading. Extend to written forms and note syllable boundary in speech and writing (W5).

● Write the characters' names on the board: Wilf, Chip, Floppy, Nadim. Say the names with the children, and clap and count the syllables.
● Ask the children to look through the story and collect words with more than two syllables in them ("pretended", "computer", "adventure").

Observing Do the children understand that the number of letters in the word is not the same as the number of syllables?

Speaking and listening activities

Objectives Use language and actions to explore and convey situations, characters and emotions (4a); create and sustain roles individually and when working with others (4b).

● Discuss the events on the red planet. Ask the children to suggest other things that might have happened, e.g. the space creatures show the children the way out, or the children take the space creatures home with them.
● Ask the children to work in groups of five or six and take the roles of Wilf, Chip, Nadim, Floppy and the space creatures.

- Tell them to choose another event for the story and act it out together.
- Ask some of the groups to act out their story for the others.

Writing

Objective To write character profiles, e.g. passports, using key words and phrases that describe or are spoken by characters in the text (T14).

- Ask the children to imagine that the characters, including Floppy, need to have a passport to travel into space.
- Model how to write a description in the form of a passport, e.g. physical features, personality traits.
- Ask them to choose one of the characters and to draw and write a passport for them.

Lost in the Jungle

Before reading

- Look at and discuss the cover with the children. Ask them to read the title and the blurb on the back cover.
- Ask them to say what they think the setting of the story will be.
- Look briefly through the story to confirm the children's ideas.

During reading

- Ask the children to read the story. Praise and encourage them while they read, and prompt as necessary.
- As you listen to individual children, ask questions about the story, for example, on page 13 ask: *How do you think the children are feeling?*

Observing Check that the children:

- ■ read high frequency words on sight (W6/7)
- ■ read with expression appropriate to the punctuation (S2).

Group and independent reading activities

Text level work

Objective To discuss story settings; to compare differences; to locate key words and phrases in the text; to consider how different settings influence and behaviour (T5).

- Discuss the settings illustrated on pages 1, 8 and 9, and 26 and 27.
- Ask the children to write a sentence describing each setting. Then the children could look through the book to find two things found only in each setting.
- Talk about how the settings in the story influence what the characters do and feel.

Observing Are the children able to find words or phrases for each setting from the text, or do they rely on the illustrations?

Sentence level work

Objective To use verb tenses with increasing accuracy in speaking and writing, and to use past tense consistently for narration (S5).

You will need to write the following sentences on the board or on sentence strips:
Biff gives Mum a plant.
Anneena comes to play.
The magic takes them to a jungle.
The children see a monkey.
They run through the jungle.
They fall into a big net.

- Discuss the verbs and their tenses in the sentences.
- Ask the children to re-write the sentences as if they were telling a story about something that has already happened, i.e. using the past tense.

Observing Are the children able to write the irregular past tense verbs "came", "took", "saw", "ran" and "fell"?

Word level work

Objective To split familiar oral and written compound words into their component parts (W4).

- Discuss how the word "birthday" on page 1 can be split into two small words.
- Ask the children to look through the text and collect other examples of compound words from the story: "greenhouse", "waterfall", "nobody", "everything".
- Can they think of any other words that have smaller words inside them?

Observing Are the children able to find words within the words?

Speaking and listening activities

Objectives Focus on the main point (1d); listen to others' reactions (2d).

- Together, talk about what sort of people the children think the explorers are. Encourage the children to each contribute one idea.
- Ask the children to work with a partner and to think about how they would describe the explorers in the story. Encourage them to use a dictionary, thesaurus or computer software to find words and phrases to describe them.
- Ask the children to share their ideas and decide which description is the most effective.

Writing

Objective To use story settings from reading, e.g. re-describe them (T13).

- Look closely together at the illustrations of the jungle in the story.
- Ask the children to suggest words that describe the features of the jungle. Draw up a list of words and phrases for the children to use.
- Ask the children to write their own descriptions of a jungle, using the illustrations and the list as a stimulus.

Cross-curricular link
◀▶ Science: Variation: compare plants and animals

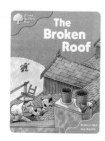

The Broken Roof

Before reading

- Look at the cover together. Can the children guess the items?
- Ask the children to read the back cover blurb and say what they think will happen in the story.

During reading

- Ask the children to read the story. Praise and encourage them while they read, and prompt as necessary.
- Encourage the children to read to the end of sentences and then return to words which cause them difficulty.

Observing Check that the children:

- read with expression appropriate to the grammar and punctuation (S2)
- use a range of strategies to work out new words such as "mangle" (T2)
- understand that this magic adventure takes the characters back in time (T5).

Group and independent reading activities

Text level work

Objective To identify and describe characters, expressing own views and using words and phrases from texts (T6).

- Ask the children to choose one of the characters from the story and to write a short description of him or her, without stating the character's name.
- Tell the children to swap their descriptions with a partner, read the descriptions and guess the name of the character.

Observing Do the children read their own descriptions to check for sense before swapping them?

Sentence level work

Objective To read aloud with intonation and expression appropriate to the grammar and punctuation (S2).

● Ask the children to work with a partner. In turn, each child reads a line of speech, using the appropriate expression, and asks "Who said this?" The partner then guesses the character, finds the spoken words in the text and points to the punctuation that shows where the speech starts and ends.

Observing Do the children change their tone when reading questions and exclamations?

Word level work

Objective To discriminate, orally, syllables in multi-syllabic words using children's names. Extend to written forms and note syllable boundary in speech and writing (W5).

● Write "Mrs May" on the board.
● Ask the children to read the name aloud and to clap the number of syllables in the name.
● Ask them to find names in the story that have one, two, three and four syllables and to write them down.
● Ask them to add other names from the class or their family that are made up of one, two, three and four syllables.

Observing Do the children count the syllables before adding other names to their lists?

Speaking and listening activities

Objectives Focus on the main point (1d); include relevant detail (1e).

● In pairs, ask the children to collaborate to draw up a list of features they see in the Victorian house, using the illustrations from pages 14 to 28.
● Ask the children to share their findings with the rest of the group and to talk about the advantages and disadvantages of living in the old house.

Writing

Objective To use story settings from reading, e.g. re-describe, use in own writing (T13).

● Discuss the illustration on pages 20 and 21 with the children. Talk about the features of the old house and write their names on the board, e.g. mangle, range, scullery, gas lamp, flat-iron.

● Ask the children to write a short description of the kitchen in the old house, using the list of words to help them. Some children could give more detail on how each feature is used.

Cross-curricular link
◄► Design & Technology: Winding Up: explore how a mangle works

The Lost Key

Before reading

- Hide the title and look at the cover with the children. Ask them to say what they think is happening.
- Read the title and ask the children to read the blurb on the back cover.
- Look briefly through the story at the illustrations. Ask the children to think about the lost key. Can they think of a reason why there are so many characters in the story?

During reading

- Ask the children to read the story. Praise and encourage them while they read, and prompt as necessary.
- Encourage the children to read with expression, pausing at commas and full stops.
- Ensure the children understand that when a line of speech is broken up, they need to continue using the same tone for the second part of the speech, e.g. "Yes," said the boys, "but we lost it again."

Observing Check that the children:

- read high frequency words with confidence (W6/7)
- know to read the direct speech with different intonation from the rest of the sentence (S2)
- use a range of strategies to work out new words (T2).

Group and independent reading activities

Text level work

Objective To predict story endings/incidents, e.g. from unfinished extracts, while reading with the teacher (T4).

- Ask the children to suggest other places where Kipper might have lost the key, e.g. the swimming pool, at school, in the shops.
- Choose one of the suggestions and make up a few opening lines, e.g. "Kipper forgot he had the key in the pocket of his swimming trunks when he went swimming. When he got dressed again, he looked in the pocket, but the key was not there. Kipper wanted to go back to the pool to look for it, but Mum wouldn't let him..."
- Ask the children, in pairs, to decide what happens next, who finds the key and how Kipper gets it back again.

- Share some of the children's ideas with the rest of the group.

Observing Do the children use the structure of the story to think of new events and outcomes?

Sentence level work

Objective To investigate and recognise a range of other ways of presenting text, e.g. speech bubbles (S7).

You will need three pieces of paper cut in the shape of speech bubbles for each child.

- Ask the children to look at the illustrations of Mum on page 25, Wilf on page 26 and Kipper on page 27, and write a speech bubble to show what each character might be saying.

Observing Do the children remember not to use speech marks in their speech bubbles?

Word level work

Objective To spell words with common prefixes, e.g. "un–", "dis–", to indicate the negative (W8).

You will need to write the following words on the board: lock, agree, appear, tie, obey, happy.

- Ask the children: *Was Kipper lucky or unlucky to lose the key? Did Mum like or dislike having to pay for the key?*
- Ask the children to write the negative form of the words on the board, by adding either "un–" or "dis–" to the beginning of each.
- Then ask the children to put the words into sentences.

Observing Do the children re-read their words to check that they sound correct?

Speaking and listening activities

Objectives Focus on the main points (1d); create and sustain roles individually and when working with others (4b).

- Look at the picture of Kipper on page 27 together.
- Choose some children to take on the role of Kipper and, in turn, sit in the "hot seat". Ask each child to describe one of the adventures he/she thinks Kipper would like to have.

Writing

Objective To use story settings from reading, e.g. re-describe, use in own writing, write a different story in the same setting (T13).

You will need to write the following questions on the board:

What did you lose?
How did you lose it?
What happened to it?
Did you find it?
How did you find it?
Was it damaged?

- Talk about some items that the children have lost, using the questions on the board as prompts.
- Ask the children to write their own story about losing something. They can use the prompts to help them to structure their writing.

Cross-curricular link
◀▶ Art & Design: Picture this: story board news report of the lost and found key

Oxford Reading Tree resources at this level

There is a range of material available at a similar level to these stories which can be used for consolidation or extension.

Stages 6 and 7

Teacher support
- Teacher's Handbook
- Guided Reading Cards for Stages 6 and 7 Stories
- Take-Home Card for each story
- Storytapes
- Stage 6–7 Workbooks 1–5
- Woodpeckers Photocopy Masters
- Group Activity Sheets Book 3 Stages 6–9
- ORT Games Stages 6–9

Further reading
- Woodpeckers Phonics Anthologies 2–5
- Playscripts Stages 6 & 7
- Fireflies Non-Fiction
- Fact Finders Units D and E
- Catkins and More Catkins Poetry

Electronic
- Clip Art
- Stage 6 & 7 Talking Stories
- ORT Online www.OxfordReadingTree.com
- Floppy and Friends

OXFORD
UNIVERSITY PRESS

Great Clarendon Street, Oxford OX2 6DP

Oxford University Press is a department of the University of Oxford. It furthers the University's objective of excellence in research, scholarship, and education by publishing worldwide in

Oxford New York

Auckland Bangkok Buenos Aires Cape Town Chennai
Dar es Salaam Delhi Hong Kong Istanbul Karachi Kolkata
Kuala Lumpur Madrid Melbourne Mexico City Mumbai Nairobi
São Paulo Shanghai Taipei Tokyo Toronto

Oxford is a registered trade mark of Oxford University Press in the UK and in certain other countries

© Oxford University Press 2003

The moral rights of the author have been asserted

Database right Oxford University Press (maker)

First published 2003

British Library Cataloguing in Publication Data

Data available

Cover illustrations Alex Brychta

Teacher's Notes: ISBN 0 19 8452233

10 9 8 7 6 5 4 3 2 1

Page make-up by IFA Design Ltd, Plymouth, Devon

Printed in Hong Kong